D0415982

Quelle Histoire
EDITIONS

Graphics: Quelle Histoire
Illustrations: Bruno Wennagel
Text: Albin Quéru and Romain Jubert

Registered office: 3, rue de Paris 75006 Fürstemberg
Editing and design: 80, rue des Haies 75020 Paris
© Quelle Histoire, Paris, 2015, all rights reserved
www.quellehistoire.com
contact@quellehistoire.fr

Manufactured by Labelfab/ Printed in France by Stin Imprimerie - Toulouse

Legal deposit october 2015

PEFC 10-31-2841/ PEFC recycled/ This product is made from recycled and controlled sources. / pefc-france.org

MADE IN FRANCE

Napoleon

Childhood

A little boy was born on August 15th, 1769 in Ajaccio on the island of Corsica. His parents, Charles and Laetizia Bonaparte named him Napoleon. They had him cross the Mediterranean Sea so he could become a soldier. At the school in Brienne he was soon made to forget his Corsican dialect and he became one of the school's best students, notably in snowball fights...

—

1769

The Bridge of Arcole

After proving himself to be a brilliant student, Napoleon became a general. He was sent to northern Italy to fight against the Austrians. On the Bridge of Arcole, he heroically led his troops into battle and won his first major victory!

———

1796

Egypt

Napoleon then left for Egypt. Upon arriving at the foot of the pyramids, he crushed the Mamluks, who were formidable warriors. He had brought along with him 200 scholars who studied the animals, plants and monuments. But, worried about what was happening back in France, he left his army and secretly boarded the ship to return to Paris.

———

1798

The Consulate

Once in Paris, Napoleon seized power and became First Consul. His achievements were immense: he re-organised the country, created new laws and schools, re-launched the currency and had monuments built to the glory of his army, like the column on the Place Vendôme in Paris... assisted by his minister Talleyrand, he even signed peace treaties with the Austrians and the English! The situation in the country improved and he was acclaimed by the people.

1799

The Coronation

Napoleon succeeded at everything he did, so he decided to become emperor...It was the 2nd of December 1804, there was a crowd at Notre-Dame; the Pope himself had come up from Rome. Going against tradition, Napoleon crowned himself. From then on he was the most powerful man in France and even in Europe. But his domination annoyed other countries. England drew closer to Austria and Russia in order to fight against him.

—

1804

Austerlitz

The English declared war on France and inflicted a terrible defeat on the French fleet at Trafalgar. The Russians and the Austrians took advantage of the situation to launch at attack in the east, but at Austerlitz, Napoleon's troops won a stunning victory: the emperor was at the summit of his glory!

———

1805

The War with Spain

In 1808, Napoleon placed his brother Joseph on the throne of Spain. The Spanish revolted and attacked French soldiers in various places around the country. The army suffered and the English gained a foothold in Spain.

1808

The Russian Rout

Then Napoleon invaded Russia. Despite the early victories, the campaign turned into a fiasco. The army could not withstand the Russian winter and had to retreat...After this terrible defeat, Napoleon's allies turned against him. On April 6th, 1819, despite fierce resistance, he was forced to abdicate and was exiled to the Isle of Elba.

1812

Waterloo

Napoleon very quickly escaped from Elba and returned to France. He rallied his army to fight against the English and the Prussians at Waterloo in Belgium. The English square formations and the Prussian cavalry thrashed the French army. Napoleon was definitively defeated.

1815

Saint Helena

The English decided to exile Napoleon to Saint Helena, a rocky island well off the beaten track, in the middle of the Atlantic. The deposed emperor would die there, alone and abandoned by his friends...

———

1821

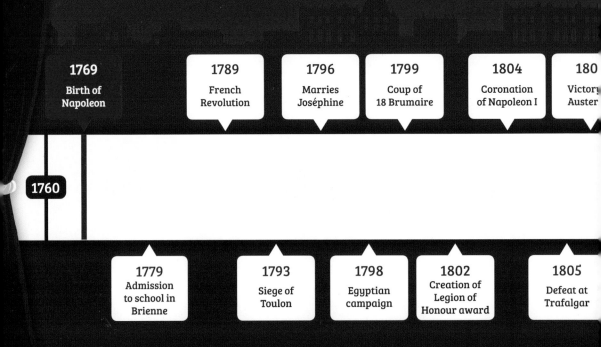

1769
Birth of Napoleon

1789
French Revolution

1796
Marries Joséphine

1799
Coup of 18 Brumaire

1804
Coronation of Napoleon I

180...
Victor...
Auster...

1760

1779
Admission to school in Brienne

1793
Siege of Toulon

1798
Egyptian campaign

1802
Creation of Legion of Honour award

1805
Defeat at Trafalgar

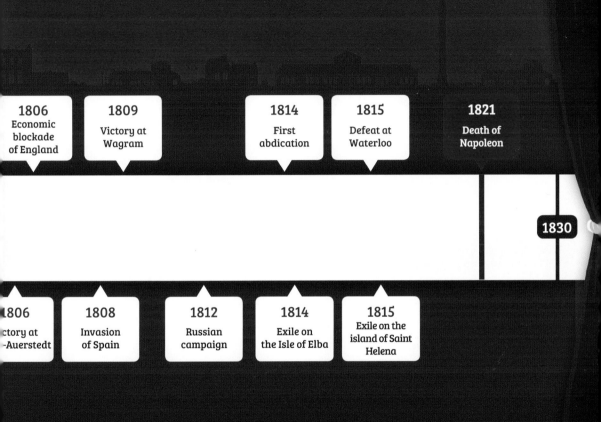

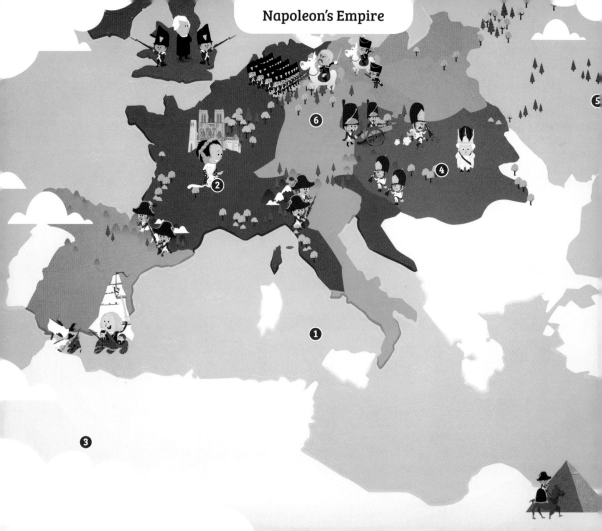

Napoleon's Empire

Key to the

MAP

 1 Ajaccio, Corsica

Napoleon was born in Ajaccio, Corsica. For a long time, he remained much attached to his native island, even planning to restore its independence!

 2 Coronation at Notre-Dame

After winning some very important battles, Napoleon decides to become French Emperor! He was crowned on December 2nd, 1804 at Notre-Dame de Paris.

 3 Battle of Trafalgar

In 1805 the British fleet attacked the French fleet at Trafalgar in southern Spain. It was an overwhelming victory for Admiral Nelson's English forces.

 4 Battle of Austerlitz

A year to the day after his coronation, Napoleon won one of the greatest battles in history, here at Austerlitz. His outnumbered army crushed the Russian army.

 5 Russian campaign

In 1812, Napoleon set out to conquer Russia. Cold, fatigue and shortages overcame his *Grande Armée*. It was a crushing defeat for the emperor.

 6 Battle of Waterloo

Having returned from exile, Napoleon tried to regain power. He confronted the British and Prussians at Waterloo. The French army was defeated in a very violent battle.

French Empire

Countries dependent on France

United Kingdom

Prussia

Austrian Empire

Russian Empire

Portraits

Josephine
(1763-1814)
Josephine met Napoleon in Paris and they got married. She was crowned Empress at Notre-Dame in 1804. She didn't manage to bear children for the emperor, who asked for a divorce.

Talleyrand
(1754-1838)
Talleyrand held a diplomatic post under Napoleon. Nicknamed the «lame devil», Talleyrand was a fascinating character, and brilliant visionary. He eventually rallied behind the cause of Louis XVIII.

Marshal Ney
(1769-1815)
Appointed marshal of France in 1804,
Ney distinguished himself in several
battles including Austerlitz and Jena.
During the terrible retreat from
Russia, he managed to save
the remnants of the army, thus
providing a rearguard.

Alexander I
(1777-1825)
Defeated by the French at Austerlitz,
Eylau and Friedland, he then moved
towards Napoleon, politically
speaking. However, in 1812, Napoleon
invaded Russia: the peace was broken
and the Tsar finally joins forces with
England and Prussia.

Game

Hunt for these pictures in the scene on the right:

Napoleon

The parrot

The sweeper

The cast
off barrel

Mummy 1

Mummy 2

Mumm

The pirate

The skier

The duck
rubber ring

The mole

The graffiti
artist

The lost
underpants

The croco

The sand
castle

The sick
camel

The swing

The ghost

The buried
man

Nelson

7 DIFFERENCES

Find the 7 differences between the left-hand and right-hand pictures

Solution: gull, scar, cufflink, moustache, badge, rifle, feather in hat

Game

MAZE

Help Napoleon find his hat

SILHOUETTES

Which one is Napoleon's silhouette?

a.

b.

c.

d.

e.

Correct answer: silhouette a

Game

QUIZ

1. Where was Napoleon born?

    a. Brittany   b. Corsica

    c. Italy   d. Paris

2. Napoleon took what/whom with him to Egypt?

    a. scholars   b. monkeys

    c. mummies   d. croissants

3. On which island was Napoleon exiled by the British?

    a. Corsica   b. Easter Island

    c. Saint Helena   d. England

Correct answers: 1.b / 2.a / 3.c

Children's History collection
for an enjoyable learning experience!

Available in bookstores in English:

Vercingetorix

Joan of Arc

Da Vinci

Francis I of France

Louis XIV

Marie-Antoinette

Discover
the Quelle Histoire apps, too!

A collection of interactive applications
to learn about history in a fun way!

For more information visit: www.quellehistoire.com

Search « Quelle Histoire » in the App Store or the App Shop